REPORT FROM THE
SEA OF MOISTURE

REPORT FROM THE SEA OF MOISTURE

Poems

STUART JAY SILVERMAN

atmosphere press

For My Wife, Sondra Rosenberg,
My Love, My Poetry

CONTENTS

III. DEAD TO RITES

IV. RECAPITULATION

IN THE DREAMTIME

INUIT MOLLUSC

So two people come out of a clamshell,
he, to the right, crawling, his butt up against her upturned belly.
He's pulling himself out with difficulty,
like a hatchling turtle crawling up from its shell
through lung-cluttering sand to the savage air
replete with gulls looking to glut their craws with turtle soup,
well, sort of, and, then, as a survivor, as may be,
on to the lovely liquid haven of the sea
to be fish fodder, perhaps, the intended
of shark and ray and similar finny terrors.

So two people break out of a clam shell,
she, to the left, not fully out, like a hatchling breaking through,
yet still half in, her long hair, by which we know her gender,
flowing under like a wave upside down, or seen upside down,
her right hand clutching the edge of the upper shell
which seems propped open on his back.
She seems to be pushing up, straining to wriggle out
held by his butt as he pushes forward,
her right arm foreshortened by the strain of pushing against.
It's not certain she'll make it despite the Inuit who say she will.

For this is a creation myth, carved from a chunk of serpentine
by Mike Pelkey, otherwise unknown to me. And these two
are the pair from which all the rest of us emerge in due course,
the primal Adam and his primordial Eve, contesting with chaos
for the world, giving birth at last to light and darkness.
So what else is new? The white bear and its prey, the seal,
slip into the waters in due course, and the waters rise along
the edge of the continents as the glaciers sink into oblivion.
For this is a creation myth, and also the beginning of the end,
time spiraling out of control grinding down the shell to dust.

CAVE SONG

here is where the boys were

i see chiba's hand, smaller than the others,
ocher still wet, his laid on gubba's fingers,
thick and tough, spring roots strong as rain,
brother to mabba, killer of stag by stabbing,
saving us from the frozentime twice past

here the small wobbly scratches
and here the woman's part
like cupped hands, one toward the sun rising
and one toward the sun setting,
between the place of seed,
the slit by which is the going in,
by which is the coming out of the newest,
the color of ocher, voice crying his spirit

in the bend of rock the antelope bells

the bull shows his horn to the hunter
the bull sniffs the wind for the hunter
his great head peering from the rock
in the ceiling vault trapping the light

there i put the horn of the rhino so rare

once on the spring plains i saw his *mana*
eating the grass flamed by father sun
followed the dung sweet with grass
down to the water where we drank as one
took of his *mana* the scent of his flanks
wet with heat in the time of the high sun
and when the sun dies into the soft line
where the eye cannot go into the night

against the pillar of rock where the cave
fades
back where the bears long gone left their
scat
i carved a woman of many breasts her
notch
heavy with longing to bear the newest
one

i was young once, like these who left hands
made by a blow of ocher beside the stag
and grandfather bull and the small small
hunter who dances beside them spear held
aloft while the spirit of the mammoth and
the stag move, the eye moving past them

light
fat in the stoup
spits out dances
around this stone
lined like a face,
old man, old woman,
close to the ending dark

i must leave the cave of spirits to the boys

i must see to the hunt, six men in the hunt
hungry, the women wait for what we bring
antelope or rabbit, or father bear, wounded
by saber cat or mammoth tusk, an easy kill

now sleep in the warmth of the woman
in the shelter of her fat in her arms her spirit

GREEK FIRE

Family failings. It is too much, or almost,
to have to put up with, with it, or them,
the archetype of them being Odysseus,
almost before the Greeks were Greeks,
before the Romans took over, and the rest,
to whom it was all Greek, anyway.
He was on his way, a touch impatient,
you might imagine, delays a tiresome
consequence of travel, sea monsters,
lotus eaters, sirens tempting as a two-day pass,
the seas a constant torment what with the sea god
spanking the monkey underwater, and what a monkey!
the size of Polyphemus puffed with pain
that time, oh you remember, the stake
sharpened and rolled in the blistering embers
until the point grew hard as bronze
and he sent it sizzling into the socket
of that fish eye, his shoulder heaving,
his hands rolling it like a spit,
the giant twisting up onto his knees
his throat torn open with the howl.
He saw by the fire a gobbet of gore
shake free to sputter like sheep fat
thrown to the gods, a sacrifice.
But what of she who waited, her
propensity to wait her only failing,
playing the woman part dangerously.
How she put the suitors off, Homer
makes much of, the wife who preserves
her honor and his, a match in cunning
to him, the fabric of her deception,
but what of it? They were a bunch of louts,
looking for an easy lay, her juices
untapped for a double decade, if rumor
had it right, the house their object,
of course, though she wasn't bad for
her age, worth a hump now and then.
In the night, as they say, and so on.

Meanwhile, there was the scar by which he
proved his being, and the bow unbent/
unstrung by the rabble infesting the hall,
its gut he hooked easily to the notch,
and the faithful hound that, despite
twenty years of wear and tear--fleas,
burs tangling his fur like wool torn
from the loom, the comings and goings
at all hours, the beggarly rags worn by the
stranger--still knew him and thumped
his tail in recognition, good doggy--
not to mention, but I must, the braggart
who'd whined and begged table scraps
and thought the stranger an easy mark,
but learned his error the hard way.
What of the neighbors? what did they
make of the usual shouts from the house
in Ithaka rising into screams, then cut
off, the dying whimper bubbling away?
They all fade into background, and
the poets fade who made the man over,
Dante sending him to hell, Tennyson
grafting him an English tongue and a
worldview worthy of an English lord,
Walcott and Kazantzakis breaking the
mold, new-fashioning the crafty hero,
all fade, and the fadings fade, and the
light rises like smoke from the pages
again and again and again, weaving
the mantle by which we lend to our
stumbling feet the semblance of gods.

FROM THE SAVANNAH CODEX*

She raises the vessel, by my own hand inscribed
Lord Of Twenty Captives, Of Copan, Of Petén
(bloodbraids falling, heads lopped from stems),

and turns it half-to-the-side letting the ropy froth
pour through fumes, muddying the cacao, bitter,
flecked brown-on-dun, cascade sacred to a Lord.

I breathe the spirit of the cacao. My hand guides
the stingray barb through my shaft, as becomes a
Lord, twists, pushing, stretching the under skin.

A spurt, the blood of the seed let loose, taking
the power of the river from the blood that drains,
fills the low-vessel, as the land drains the river.

The Lord Who Was My Father nods in the mist,
who held the Jaguar on the might of his shield,
and She-who-bears-the-vessel, and is My Lady,

lets a ribbon of blood from her tongue, twists
the jade point midway between lip and voice.
Thus, the fields are made fertile, the bodies of

our enemies weaken, the Rain God tears at his
breast to water my land, the sacrifice made is
accepted, gods drunken with the fall of blood.

So, I enter into my dream. Rabbit nibbles a root,
Eagle buries its hooked beak in an opened chest,
a captive Chief, smoke ripples the roof of the cave;

through the long night the snake flings out coils
of darkness swollen by the blood-letting, ripples
on which he rises, eyes shadowed by the light.

I am here three days, in the cave of my mind,
seeing the days pace the overhead night of stars,
Gods gone beyond the need for blood, old gods,

Xipe, flayed skin a tunic tough as smoked rubber,
the Maize God, filling the seed filling the land,
Xoc, scourge of the waters girdling the world,

and come back, the Sun God flooding, filling
the mouth of the cave, light a froth of cacao,
froth green-and-gold feathering the skin, and I,

graven by the light of the long-tailed Quetzal,
return into my consort; so, together, we return
the seed to the warm dark, warmed by blood,
where She bears for our House its next Lord.

*It might be worth noting that there is no Savannah Codex,
as befits a fantasy based on *Breaking the Maya Code* by
Michael D. Coe.

THE ORKNEYS, AN ODYSSEY

On the map, blobs of yellow
beat north from
Duncansby Head
into the blue sea-froth.

A scud of wet, flopping of sea,
chops at the islands
up from Scapa Flow,
Stronsay to N. Ronaldsay.

At the local, in Kirkwatt,
syllables mashed like swedes   [rutabagas]
clump on the board.
The whiskey boasts of the sea.

I hear a scrape
of sea-floor scree
under the cliff-head
facing north at Rousay,

see the sea push up
at the winds from round the head,
listen to the wash of waves
against the staring sands.

"They came here, the Greeks,"
a sea-man on sea-raked beach
says. "That seal head's
Circe, peeping through waves."

The landlord brings out
a pebble of brass
found on the shore.
"Phoenician work, that," he says.

Button or brooch,
it keeps its mystery,
too worn to prattle,
not faith, not fashioning.

ANOTHER LIFE

Six hours south of the border of Texas--
Cuatro Ciénagas lies at ease in the sand.
Spring-fed, deep in the heart of *Chihuahua*,
oases stare up at the sweltering sun.
Skinners cinched packs for the haul to the lead mines
where dust-swimming light fades the light in each eye.

Eye-blue the pools stand, in *Cuatro Ciénagas*,
deep-ribbed, the lilies afloat on each pool.
The desert sun shading from saffron to purple
skids in its glide a long way to the west.
A sidewinder whips through an alley of maguey,
tongue quick with the scent of a kangaroo rat.

Nearby, a scorpion arches its backplates,
a glitter of chitin half lost in the sand.
The lemon-streaked white-and-rose of the water plants
gives up the ghost to a sharp edge of night.
Now a coyote's brief undulant howls
with the softening hoots of an owl change place.

Near where a footprint hides under the sand,
blown by a whimsical stutter of wind,
silence envelops the blanketing air
which cools its heels at the loblolly pine
while the moon rides its arc over the desert
past derelict stars trapped in the sky.

THE LONG VIEW

when lava began to flow down the slopes of Vesuvius in 79 A.D.
becoming folds of dark velvet streaked crimson, the ashen top layers
crinkling, opening onto the inferno's incandescent offspring which
flow the surface ruffling and puffing shards of sulfur-stinging gas
to the roiling air,
           a peasant up from the town and first to die, heart-
strings twisted into knots by the fury gods must have sent out into
the wavering light, his gaunt body consumed almost too quick for
pain by the molten eructation softening the tufa of old eruptions
which will harden to stone again and lie doggo in the aftermath,

was looking for a rare bird, black with an ivory beak, a red crest
like the plumes an emperor might wear at the head of a column,
his men in ceremonial armor throwing back the sun when noon
crept along the cobbled street, prisoners a square of human
waste prodded into movement, eyes glittering with the gold coin
promised and the girls promised and the scent of thyme in the air

but all that is lost in the swirling clouds of choking gas; the stone
ocean seethes in the morning and afternoon and sends a froth of
fire into the night, and, below, the town gives up the fight, mothers
petrified, children struggling to be free of the arm and the breast
which cannot shelter them from the terror riding over the roofs
into the rooms, down narrow halls and over gilt-trimmed wood,
into the cisterns and the cloaca, making itself a home while
the streets flow with senator and slave, wives and whores, a dog
true to its master as it becomes a mold that reeks of burnt hair,
two kids meant for a meal, the ruck and wrack of a civilization,
a city passing into history, a stone poem, text ripe for exegesis.

This is the long view for us, we who are left with the frozen
sarcophagus of what went on, not memory but a shadow of one,
place dissolving into time, the table cleared of all but scraps,
a stone wall holding in nothing, the charred outline of something.

VALERY REFRACTED

Tout le ciel vert se meurt. Le dernier arbre brûle.

All the green sky is dying. The last tree flames
capturing the sun in arms which hang, like poppies
drenching a field in scarlet robes. The sky fights
free of heaven, the final hope, sanctuary from which
we scatter among the bleating animals desperate for
comfort, which we cannot conceive, having outlived
our lives. Dust breaks in a clump from a root that
undercuts this river bank whose mud trickle meanders
down a last minim of channel.
>   *(No. It is not true.)*

We rise into the green light cleansed of body, as if a
dream commandeered its dreamers and drove them before it
into the dawning sun.
>   *(No. None of it is true.)*

We are not here. Only our fear has come before us to this end
where the green sky puffs out its final breath while
the last tree waves a bouffant of flame at the sun,
its dead root breaking out of the slant bank as
though reaching for water that will give it life.
>   *(And this is true.)*

AT THE BORDER

I've been told that the past is a foreign country,
yet though I'm a citizen of the present I've been there.
Not recently, of course, and mostly not: a border,
here and there mainly a few towns and villages
where people I thought I knew fail to recognize me.
The streets lean toward the houses that squint up,
look past wisps of gray which hide a ragged sun.

In the town hall of the capital the archives are closed
to all but the most austere puzzlers turning over pages.
They've been told these house the history of the place.
The backs of their heads nod in agreement crafting
the time they will carry back to their own countries,
as precious as breath, and use to fill in the empty
space that has dispossessed them of palpable being.

You must go by way of the lost rivers of time, which,
by the way, do not exist, except as poetry, as words,
fending off the chimeras that inhabit the place:
the lost loves divested of memory and strangely distorted,
youthful peccadilloes and adventures invented for later on,
for when you have lived long enough to yearn to return
to the hollow from which you imagine you once emerged.

And what of that return, fording the hurtling waters,
speaking to no one, or, if you speak, resigned to silence,
the words taken away by the desperate hills and desolate
valleys you thought you had left forever? What of
the slag heaps of bridges you burned, which exist only
as signposts in a world uncertain of existence?
What of the questions you have forgotten how to ask?

WHAT WE SEE

There she goes, or he, steady as a snail,
a round red drunk leering over a fence.
Night is just around the corner. A trail
of light wanders over the unseen grass
while the moon whitens and crickets untense.
It is as though the coming has come to pass,
and meaning soon will break into being,
but nothing of that is what we're seeing.
Wisdom doesn't erupt into the clear.
The moon never wavers inching up the sky,
her round face curding to yellowish whey.
Nothing more. Star ghosts reliably steer
as starry-eyed their hosts did in their day
until their fuel cells emptied with a sigh.

MUDWOMEN

I've been looking at a postcard of two mudwomen (copyright 1997) and
thinking that for mudwomen they are alright, by which I mean all right, a
correction I make only to placate the cybergods who have taken to
underlining words in red (for example, cybergods), to call them to my
attention. I presume something is wrong with these words, which are
unpleasing to my machine, which, unlike me, comes straight out with an
opinion. about the mudwomen, however, the machine has no opinion,
not having, after all, the requisite optical equipment for picking up the
photons that bounce back from the postcard, or so I imagine, as the card,
which checks in at, oh, a thirtieth of an inch, couldn't possibly conceal
two women within its narrow interior, not even women only 3 1/2 inches
high, one whose arms cross beneath her breasts, symmetrical and plump,
if no more than a B-cup, the other standing left arm akimbo on her hip,
making a pumphandle angle away from her body, her right hand hiding
behind her friend's back, reassuring, perhaps, while her breasts, which
tend toward a C-cup, hang down asymmetrically, the left a tad flattened,
drooping a hand breadth lower than the distinctly smaller one on the
right. so here I am looking at a postcard of two half-naked women as
though I were fourteen again and peering at underwear ads in the
women's magazines of my youth, and ignoring the mud masks which are
surely the distinctive feature of the image. the masks suggest new guinea,
sepik or black river, perhaps, if I may be allowed to show off just a little,
but the women's bodies are white, white despite the artistically-arranged
daubs of mud looking like tattoos that occupy, at a guess, 10% of the
visible skin, meaning the portion not around the pelvis, which is covered
with flaps of cloth strung onto a cord looped around each waist. what I'm
looking at is a single frame of film showing the negative's perf marks at
the top and presenting what appears to be a box, its floor a scuffed
canvas, within which the women stand. it might be an homage to the
studio photo circa 1890, the women models, the intention to titillate,
white women posed like exploited native women for the delectation of
the modern voyeur, the mud masks radically fetishizing the human,
transforming it into an object of desire and repulsion, the dark space
within which the women stand, a place Conrad might have found for
churning the dark tidal waters of the unconscious. they face out of the
picture as though challenging the viewer, one mask slashed by a mouth
in which a double line of teeth leaning to our left makes a serrated dash
across the face, one a tooth-jagged oval, both with boar's tusks through

the septum, and, under, the breasts, the breasts heavy with magic, in the composition moving on a plane, each crucified on the abscissa of the imagination but, probably, needing the money, sacrificing the niceties and not having anything better, and being persuaded what they were doing would be art, or ART, and aware that the masks made it impossible for anyone to recognize them absent lover or doctor, surrendered to the insistent lens. my hands form hammocks to cradle the breasts of the one on the right, the one of the lopsided breasts and tiny aureoles and nipples like starfish fastened onto the flattered skin. I am lost in her, her image frozen into the flat plane of the card, her being being the life she has, I hope, somewhere beyond the artifice imposed, her fictive being echoing an anima in which she always lives beyond our reach.

TRIP(PING THE LIGHT FANTAS)TIC

Inside the atlas, where Ireland, north and south,
eddies through the slop, St. George's Channel,
where the wash of the Irish Sea battles
the Atlantic furies back through a sluice
of deep water, the ridge of wet sloshing between
Bangor and Portpatric, I can taste the land,
the sheepfolds on cotter's farms in Longford,
hung wash whipped to a froth over wet grass,
a land of snug square carpets tamped down by mist,
raw wool, tough as fishline, runes spellbound
beside the sea at Ballyhannon, a peat fire
smoking stoneside and thatchtop at Kilkee,
north of Loop Head, and the sea-burnt cottager
beside the leaning gray wood of a stile,
clay pipe fitted in place as though forever,
who knocks the dottle wetly into the road
turning back to the pages of his life,
closed to me, always somewhere else.

A DREAM OF BORGES

as told by a passerby

In an obscure corner of Patagonia, which is, all considered,
sunk in obscurity, and in a remote lozenge of land in its embrace,
and, in a way, distinguished by its low-lying soil covered by
grass, moss-darkened by rain in the late-Fall, bled yellow-and-ochre
by sun in the dry months, a disciple of Borges established a place
of rest and meditation according to the master's principles.

The Echo Museum, as it came to be known, like the logarithmic
spiral of a nautilus shell, emerged, at last, into the light, a series of
rooms, or interior spaces, occupied by the susurration of history,
the aphorisms, apothegms, axioms, and animadversions of the
saints and sinners, the quibblers and quixotics, the madmen and
madder women who invest the ages and pass away but leave a
legacy of crotchety maxims and blurted wisdom for the hordes
to ponder in their own time. These were given existence in perpetuity
not by a flux of electrons, or lines braided from magnetic fields,
or, *a fortiori*, by a succession of smeared or gouged marks left
by chalk or stylus, but as reverberant acoustic waves propagated
from curve to melting curve in interlocking chambers too convoluted
for the lens to contain or the optic nerve to pass on or the imagination
to intuit, however perspicuous to the attentive ear.

The casual auditor, stand where he or she might, heard only
the whistle of untethered winds, or a confusion of sea-frothed waves
slapping at the bent wood of a lightly-freighted ship, or, so they said,
a memory of Babel, the articulations of a barbarous multitude,
none intelligible past the boundaries of its individual progenitor.

Yet, for some few, the walls of the labyrinth themselves appeared
to move. Undulant as anemone or that naked mollusk, the octopus,
they carried to the chosen ear a fragment of the *Timaeus,* Portia's harsh
rebuke of Shylock, the musings of Einstein challenging a god who,
it seemed likely, played dice with the universe, and numerous unknown
others. When these favored few emerged, silent for a long moment,
in the sensible air, as though upon a peak in Darien, they would each
ask the same question: "Why can I remember nothing?"

For it was a strange property of the interior echo that its trace
unraveled on exposure to the outer world taking with it into the abyss
of nothingness a train of skittish protocerebrations, fractured notions,
the husks of dreams, a chaff of axonic debris fluttering just beyond

grasp like Hamlin's unfortunate mice and more unfortunate children.

Only shadows remained of the voices and of those who had heard them, or claimed to have done so, for among those who made no such claim, who could, with the least hope of success, prove, or disprove, the being of the phantoms that beguiled and bedeviled a residuum of the chosen?

And, in time, fabulous rumors, strange to tell, of a new structure, somewhere in the pampas, west of *gaucho,* if somewhat east of *guaso,* arose, a citadel to the master's memory, each stone and wisp of mortar a revenant rising on thermals of condor-winged thought. It was called The Shadow Museum.

I learned of this curiosity, which, it's necessary to add, no longer exists, for reasons I hope to explain another time, on a visit to it during its impossible tenure. There, for a while, amid the shades of Persia and Pompeii, the ambiguities of the to-be civilization that will rise along the north shore of Cassiopeia's Lake of Mysteries, the quantum-froth on which Cockaigne's apotheosis rests for all eternity, the museum held its own with existence for a short spell.

There, in thrall to time and space on their longwinded rebarbative journeyings, shadows of what might be gave an illusory comfort to the mind wandering through a concourse empty of what was, and paid due homage to the thought that may have flickered a while in that twilight of worlds. And, in the half-existence vouchsafed the mind during its final spin out toward oblivion, I believe, a flicker of that phantasm still makes a random walk, tramps the lattice which mind flings into the void, neither great nor little, for dimension is without meaning within that curious increment of being, with body hovering on the edge of...

THE ROOM, THE PAINTING, AND THE LIGHT

For a few hours each morning, the sun shone through a
lattice of narrow wooden laths on the east side of the house
and, slowed imperceptibly by a sheet of window glass, moved
across space still empty of people and onto the flat plane
of a painting hanging on the wall of the opposed foyer.

When he was up early, he sat in the room with the window
watching the puddle of light flow across the heart pine floor
at the edge of the foyer, and from there cross to the base of
the wall on which the picture hung, and from there turn up,
as though feeling for the picture waiting for its arrival.

Then, the light would hesitate, the sun risen above the
aperture of the window, or it blossomed, he thought, filling
the room opposed and the foyer where it was caught by dust and
thrown into his eyes as a cluster of stars, and, then, it was throughout,
and morning took incurious possession of the room.

WILLOW

She said, "I am a tree
whose branches explore the air
feeling for the sky."

She spoke to the bird
nesting halfway up thinking
her a tree.

The wind laid hands
on the bark that fit her
like a glove

and made a soft sound
to which the bird replied
while she wept.

Her roots hid under
her eyes. She sank into the
welcoming earth

which held her
while the clouds gathered
beating back the sun.

The worms and beetles,
used to her ways, make space
for her entering parts.

She takes the rain to heart
that pelts the earth
like a childish wish.

She becomes herself
as she always
wished to be.

SEAMS

I put on my pants,
for what was it, the hundredth,
the hundred-thousandth time?

The same old pants,
smelly with farts and
food fallen from lap trays.

They have to last,
like old friends, until
I can make new ones appear

out of the air, out of
the hope that abandons me,
like a flotilla

on a widening sea,
the shore, long out of sight,
a fracture in the mind.

THE ICEBERG

in Patagonia lay back
against the water, floe against flow,
rivery-blue where it had split
from a mountain of ice,
split from its mother
to sail the southern ocean
to the edge of the land
leading to the pole.

Now its lonely self,
carves a bow wave
like a scoop of ice cream
out of the shadowy giant
in which it harbors
whose gelid feet wash the sea floor
that juts from the shelving land.

For us, the sea is a blanket of mist
muffling sound beyond the rail.
Not even a mew of seabirds--but
a creak of tackle startles the air,
a metallic clank, a tired shoe
measuring this blank plank deck.

We dream the ship is anchored,
the water holding it steady.
We dream we have been dreaming
that the ship floats on an oily sea,
that however far we drift
we are never far from Patagonia.
We wake to a bare expanse of rock
off the port bow welcoming us back
from whatever where we were.

Dawn spreads its fuzzy light across
a sea frowsy with dreams.

Next, we steer north for Valparaiso.

MOONING PSYCHE

JACOB AND MOLLY

old Jacob looked up from the bed near the window
and wondered aloud whether it was okay for him
to come into her, his wife, Molly, who laid aside
the magazine she'd been reading and nodded yes.
men had need to come into a woman, now-and-then,
she knew, and moved a little to the wall side
so he could slide over beside her and lift her
nightgown up away from her breasts, their slack
folds slumped against her chest. they had once been
full, he thought, whose pale nipples hardly dented
the surface from out of which they'd pushed in the
early days of their marriage when she was nursing
Eliot, their first-born. he cupped one in his hand and
bent his head to lip around the onion-skin patch of
light purple though he knew nothing would shiver
in her loins. he ran his tongue around her right bubby
and then her left until he felt his putz harden. she
found his tongue not so much a nuisance, as, she
thought, unnecessary, but if it made him happy she
would not tell him to stop. then, he moved down her
belly, heavy like a stuffed derma, but smooth and
white despite her years, and--what else did a Jew
need for his Jewish beak?--rubbed her hairy patch
at the front where the baby-pink under-nose hid. if
she felt something, she didn't indicate it, but lay
breathing evenly while he got on with it. so he
parted her legs a bit more and she raised them to
let him in and he rested on his knees and his left
hand while with his right hand he moistened his
thing with saliva and wedged the head and stubby
body into her, wiggling to get it all the way in. not
that its five inches was a problem. she could have
taken twice as much, he knew, having seen her
engulf a Hebrew National once when she'd left
the bathroom door half open thinking she was
alone, but he'd come home early and saw her,
the sausage between her legs, and heard the gasps
she let out turn to a long squeal tapering to a sigh

almost like a sob while he backed away silently.
he walked around the block a few times before
he walked in noisily and met her as she came to
meet him wearing a housecoat and carrying a
dust cloth, her face red and puffy, as though from
housework. he was short, Jacob thought, as he
worked it from side to side, but thick, the head
heavy as the ass of a turkey, what his son called
"the pope's nose" and it felt good inside her cave,
which was slick, now, her juice and his mingled,
and he moved tentatively faster, pushing it as far
as it would go thinking of Deborah, who had shown
him how to do it when her mother was shopping
one afternoon, and it rode smooth into her vault
and he said "is it okay?" and his wife said "okay"
thinking "he's like a sack of flour on me, a sack
rubbing against me, a child happy playing with
his pee pee; it gives him pleasure, so why not?"
then, as he was about to come, he held back
savoring the sweet sense of just lying there on
her soft belly, her depths holding him as they
did on their honeymoon, when she rode him
happily thinking of the children his putz in her
would bring into being to bring them nachus
in their now old age. she feels him shudder,
accepting the wetness flowing through the
valley of her cunt which will not flower again
though it brings him this fulfillment. he relaxes
into the flow that goes out of him warmed by
Deborah, the memory of her, into Molly, and
as he dies, leasing his power, he is unsure
whose body he has taken for his own, or who
has gathered him to her, his worn manhood
into her warm halls, and she lies under him,
comforted, though she's never quite sure why.

ZOO STORY

see the rabbi in the black hat taking the children to the zoo
he wears a white beard under his black hat, see?
over there is the giraffe taller even than the rabbi
but the giraffe lives in the zoo
and chews its cud
and has cloven hooves like a cow which also chews its cud
and like a horse which however does not chew its cud
which the rabbi tells the children to remember
the giraffe stands tall not because of pride
what is there to be proud of?
but because a giraffe is tall just as a rabbi wears a black hat
just as a rabbi taking the children to the zoo has a white beard
the next cage houses a camel and another camel and a llama
about which ogden nash wrote a few verses featuring a lama
and also a silk pajama which unfortunately the rabbi hasn't read
it's not in the middrash so in any case it isn't important
the children gather around the rabbi to hear him talk about torah
and about how animals are given respect as are women
and kosher refers to more than just the meat we eat
which explains the mikvah and the animals are well fed
notice the lions and panthers are not allowed near the camels
and do not put your hands through the bars of the cages
which protect the animals from the people as well as the other way
the marmosets staring up from their fruit held in paws like hands
the birds whose feathers glow like plasma
yellow like mustard hiding a *tref* red *putz* pillowed in a bun
that they see people wolfing down and in the next cage a wolf lounges
against the concrete slab it shares with a she-wolf and his *putz* is red
as the hot dog in its chiffon of gassy dough and next the polar bear
bobbing in the pool thoughtfully provided for it and
the children pointing now to where
with urgent paws she is clambering out
and disappearing into her house the drops making a trail that stays
lapping up the sun after she has swayed into the dark opening
and the rabbi is buying the kids an ice cream
which is kosher he tells them buying one for each saying
look for the *heckshah* on the paper you peel down to expose the cream
and you can have a Hebrew National after it but not ice cream after *fleisch*

even Hebrew National because that's the Law and he says it so the capital
L
hangs in the air
and in the next cage the sloth hangs by its tail from a branch
and in the next cage a leopard pants on a stone slab in the heat
that seeps in through the bars from the sun studying the scene
but there is no next cage
only a building made of gray cement without windows
in which in dim light a Burmese python coils around a branch
and at the end of which something called a *fer de lance*
lies invisibly in a pile of brush and the smell wrinkles up the faces
staring through unclear glass and going into a place where a tarantula
stares back from a box set into the wall and a scorpion
back arched, stinger on the ready behind the heavy glass
and so out into the air thank you they say and the rabbi nods
so off they go to get the train that will take them back to Crown Heights
where they will repeat after the rabbi their aleph beyt gimmel dalet
from which the word *alphabet* emerges
a linguistic Venus as it were and the animals pace about their enclosures
or look out of the shadows in which they have hidden
to where the light ebbs and wanes
the water comes to wash
the food comes to feed
the people come to
wander past

IN THE SUPERMARKET

the young couple with the baby
walks up and down the aisles

he sniffs the air eyes turned in
seeing the stone bridge over

the Neva water rushing along
as though it had somewhere to be

there are canned goods here
heavy as plutonium heavier

than the gold rubles she paid
to the border guard who said

go now so they went and came
to where they walk up and down

the meat in its plastic shawl
leers so they take one package

then another then another
her blouse heavy with meat

if the baby pinched cries at the
checkout it has done its job

his pockets sweetened by bars
marked snickers mars bazooka

go unnoticed by the nice lady
who is so fat she must be rich

they are all rich my father knew
he told us go the streets run with

cars the poor wear sable they are
fat and stupid but dollars drip

from their mouths like spit the
pears do not ripen but rot in bins

they have a car in the lot where
streets run with dollars her eyes

opening a sun dusty and heavy
as the baby she carried in her

when the guard took the gold and
when she bent while he searched

there is not enough here for what
he took but the baby cries and

they have escaped once more
to the waiting car and the streets

on which gold cold and heavy
gives itself indifferently to all

FISHING

later I went to bed
but thought about everything we'd spoken of
and the night happened to be long
summer having set in somewhat early
so it seemed

and mulled over,
as if it were wine, maybe, as if it had happened
more than once in the fungible past
when we had proper winters and were up early
to fire the stove

but father had
been up before us, of course, as was natural,
while in my *now* the night outside is
nagging at memory while a sorrowing bird
niggling beyond

the window joist
fills me with well not exactly fills me, no,
but makes me *feel* filled to a brim
as though flesh might sport a brim
upset like a cup

so when I left
the bed's lumps and sags for the kitchen
frowsy with morning light and
started the coffee going in the machine
I remembered

the dream the one
in which daddy woke me at four a.m. as
he had those years gone these
many years and fingers crossed fired up
the cranky Ford

to sail through the
dawning streets grumpily getting ready
the people shambling ghost-like
through the graveyard city off to work
and we to the bay

slick with discharge
where once sheepshead crowded the piles
sunk fifty feet under which now felt
only the wrack and rind of an aging city
in slow decay

and we chugged far
into the near Atlantic seaways watching
light glance off waves like shingles
till porgy and blackfish came up to us
out of the wet

to fill burlap
with flesh tiled over by scales slick as snot
to be humped onto the gangway
up to the dock leaking blood into the rear well,
rumpling a paper.

so we spoke of
the neighbors who would no longer take
a gift of fish, they smarter than the
citizens of Troy (Greece, *pas* New York),
poor man, he who

would not eat fish,
not even those he'd caught in the early light
and afternoon and lugged happily back
to show off and I trailed behind as always
vaguely satisfied,

tired, eating the
cheese sandwich the tuna fish sandwich the
hard boiled egg banana Devil Dog
whatever had survived our hunger earlier
our eyes intent

on the water and
the chum thrown from the bow then floating
to the stern and the puke nudged by
condoms like corpse-white jellyfish drifting
with the effluent

of the city miles
back where we left it huddled away from the
harbor where things begin and end
and I recalled these things on a summer night
dreaming myself

still that other,
shadow to the old man stalking his dank vision,
a whisper of being peeled from the old man.
we live now in the dreams I drag into the light
gut-hooked, snagged

willy-nilly
from the dark Atlantic of our own calendar, ripped
page by page from the coiled spiral
on which our days and nights depend winter and spring
summer and fall

fishing out the
overabundance that plumps the burlap stiffening to
deadweight, clots of gurry we must drag
across concrete to the waiting car heavy as stories,
heavy as night

YOUR PALACE, OR MINE?

When the Duke of ______ rode to hounds,
his concern was not for the alleys of dark pine
and the difficult bird life he had commissioned
some Italian to limn for his keeping in a book,
every feather to be just so, the hawk eye not
that Prussian blue he had seen when visiting
the Swedish king, but a solid marmoreal black
inky as soot passed through the bladder of a
hog and washed in a virgin's tears. He was
a man of desires, and the illusions of his house,
which was one of the oldest in Saxony, and
which, despite its many defeats, and the loss
of territory and prestige and, most important,
power, held its metaphorical head high, and
married off its daughters, as well as it could,
the girls fortunately comely, and well-endowed
with womanly wiles, if not otherwise. So on
the name day of his youngest daughter, Inger,
he gave it out that a prince of the Letts had
proposed a union of their houses and, as well,
the hand of Inger, to cement the relation and
bind two families of impeccable lineage for
the benefit of both.   An unfortunate lacuna
occurs, alas, in the manuscript. Some ascribe it
to fire, which might, indeed, have seared a path
across the vellum. Scholars attribute the lack
of scorch marks to later scribal hands, which,
perhaps, excised the burn producing the line
like a draftsman's curve which defaces a page
here and there of the original. Not that we
possess the original, let me quickly add.
Though the vellum is authentic 15th century
manufacture, it is a palimpsest of time, words
and, perhaps, whole passages having been
scraped from the surface. And no one is sure
how many such sheets were copied from sheets
damaged beyond repair by insects spawned
by the night damps of the ancestral library,

the gnawings of rodents, or their droppings,
the faulty vision or palsied hands of scribes
shut away from the light of day for their
entire unnatural lives. Thus, the history of
the House of _____, and of the Duke's last
issue, has come down to us only as hints,
mere shadows of the flesh that would fart
feasting in the Great Hall, the trysts and
trials, whispers and trumpetings, the bloated
pageants, the lashings, the dungeons whose
walls gave no sign of the routine horrors
they enclosed as a matter of course, and, of
course, of right, nor of the *droit du seigneur*
still occasionally exercised as late as the last
century, though no one would publicly aver.
These gaps being the case, as the Austrian
philosopher, in his disquisitions on the real,
would have it, the story has no conclusion,
fiction being, in that way, unlike being,
the happenstance which exhibits finitude
with boring regularity, whether among the
high and mighty or the lowest beetle
skittering among the rafts of pond slime
gathered in the long abandoned depths
of the ancient and enduring ducal moat.
Only by a trick of light on a few otherwise
unnotable faces noticed in shops or elbowed
without a glance on pavement or path or
seen waiting, the eternal *bourgeois*, for
a tax stamp or official seal on a document
needed to exist in the town of ______,
will the eye discern a troubling angle of jaw,
shading of cheekbone, and call to mind the
portrait of the Duke in the museum now open
to the public for a small fee on a daily basis.
It should be mentioned that the management
offers a buffet luncheon in the garden terrace,
credit cards not accepted. Photography,
sans flash, permitted in the newly restored
public rooms.

A HILLSIDE IN WALES

It was Ginsberg, I swear, I saw that day,
aloft on a cloud, his eyes scattering light
crepitant as peanut shells. I watched them
eddy downwards teasing the breathless wind.
On his right, Corso floated, flatulent as a frog,
a frog insufflated by a bad boy *sans* scruples
who was wielding a bicycle pump, a pump
pumping away, 80% nitrogen, the rest mostly
oxygen, with a smidgen of noble gases and
a miscellany of methane and carbon dioxide,
flotsam and jetsam of the lower atmosphere.
Knowledge, after all, is power, we're told.

Al was putting his queer left shoulder to,
if not the wheel, then to the biker beside him,
leathers polished by sun to a simulacrum
of the shield Hephaestus cobbled up on his forge.
He made it for headstrong Achilles, the hero,
always champing at the bit to put the boot in,
not too smart, you might say, our boy,
but great to have at your back in a rumble.

The vision held. So, a puddle slick with oil
may, for the moment, be a prism and center
a rainbow in the lubricant lens filming its
watery flux.
            It held while a dusty bee
circled in meditation a timeless moment
considering the myriad daffodils littering
the green, *along a green crag glimpsed through
mullioned glass*, so he wrote.
            And it might almost have been.

When I looked up, a phalanx of empty clouds
stood picket; a captive blue circumambulating
a sky which hovered properly overhead but
vacuous as a palimpsest muzzy with lost words.

Later in the week, I saw him slouching again.
He took up a position against a megalith
whose plinth, half sunk in grass-smeared earth,
looked to the east

as though to avoid the darkening hills
which made a jacket for the dying sun.

A BATTLE AT SEA

What did he think, the sailor-warrior
camped aloft brandishing a spear
while the pirate-Greeks came on,
prow splitting the calm Tyrhene?

Was it the purple wine, thinned to a sun-lit puce
by water from a hidden spring,
that he drank in the cool shade of an arbutus
on the flagstones ringing the temple walls?

Did he fear the fall to the plank deck
or a two-edged spear point
embedded in breastbone, the lucky pitch
of a helmed Greek a ships-breadth away?

He sways in the mind across the centuries,
a stick-man almost lost above the battle
ended one way or the other in the fabulous ago.

Neither the scholars parsing his kind with a patient care,
nor the poets building a world in which he might exist once more,
can find a way to the heart of his mystery.

> *A hunter, doomed by a glimpse, no more,*
> *but more than the gods sanctioned, then or now,*
> *of what time and fate hide from human eyes,*
> *left his blood on the Thessalian plains.*
> *Torn by the hounds who saw only the stag,*
> *he has become the myth of afterwards.*

All that remains of the Etruscan sailor
is perched on the clay of the Aristonothos Crater.

Not even the enigmatic Etruscan smile
humanizes the challenge of this earth.

SEADRIFT
A Cento

"Be careful of open waters, it's said, more
than the trafficked lanes of shipping:
in those, the problem is perspicuous, and
avoidable, and the vessels' masters are
alert to your incursions as you to theirs."

"Harbor no ill thoughts, which corrupt the soul.
Steer to the calm waters that buoy the lapped
strakes. Trust to the deep and weighty keel to
keep you aright over the dark, abiding sea."

"Adrift in the vast ocean, a dreadnaught no less
than a pinnace must surrender itself to chance.
Survival depends on forces no sailor can fathom."

"An ocean of mist swallowed up the sky. Our faces
wet at the masthead no less than by the helm, we
tacked against what little breeze stirred, like a
blind man feeling his way through a strange room."

"Wind stripped the rigging from the mainmast and
cleared the deck of a marlinspike left carelessly
loose. I saw it thrown like a used toothpick
into the air, and driven into the forward bulkhead
four inches, as determined by measurement later
when we had cleared the horn and lay to in a brief
calm to survey damage and make good what we could."

"Higgins slipped over the side crazy with heat and
thirst saying he would rather be salt pickled than
a spindle of dried beef. Hardly had the words been
uttered before a look of amazement creased his face,
and, then, a strange gurgling sound, like a drain,
its plug pulled, and the water heaved. He began to
slip away and, so, we hauled him up, surprising
light, it seemed, and there was only the half, the
bottom sheared away like a mullet snapped in two.

Three days later a French frigate had the kindness
to pick us out of the water. We was then exchanged
for a complement of Frogs as we lay to, under flag
of truce, to take on water in the roads at New Georgia."

"I've swum with sharks without incident, but, then,
I think they weren't hungry what with the numbers
of bodies idling in the water after we went down."

"When they took off my leg, I had above two pints of
grog in me, and Stevens, the bosun's mate did me the
kindness of a tap on the side of my head with his
belaying pin, so I hardly remember what I felt aside
from the steady sound of the saw parting the bone
and the crackle of hot tar sealing off the stump."

"We come from the sea, its brine courses through our
veins and arteries, its memory lingers in the tissue
and returns to the tides when the land has done with
the husks and hulls that cumber the indigent being."

MARSHLANDS

"a river of leaves, swollen by subaqueous feelings,"
as Quasimodo might have written,
conscious of the *Val Borgo di Taro*
and the eponymous sea-seeking river
and the shoreline along the Ligurian Sea,
but didn't, though he wrote of marshlands
and the slumbrous south,
and of *"acqua allarga/il ricordoi suoi anelli,"*
by which he means memory
widening in rings as though on water,
and ignores the barbarous tribes
so long ago in a constant frisson of war,
and the troops sweating moving up towards the Apennines
back in '44, beating off the flies and mosquitoes,
malaria and diarrhea as much a danger as Il Duce,
whose dead body stripped of *genitali*
hung from a lamppost for two days
so the mob could taunt a memory
of suffering real and imagined,
but returns to the sea, to the saline mystery of the estuary,
the ilex and poplar,
what lasts though defeated by time and weather,
blood making a riverbed of our bodies,
the salt heat of summer when the wind
fades to memory caught in fragments of sea coast
and in the distance the horizon takes over.

A BLOOMSBURY PORTRAIT

"He was always the last to leave,
after the bottom of the punch bowl
had given up its final honeyed sip.
He half-leaned against the bolster
for a time. If he spoke further,
his voice crept by in a whisper,
as though aware that an emptiness
had sunk in on which words intrude.
Then, if he spoke, he would look
toward the grape-and-dart molding
high up the wall where words might,
perhaps, escape attention and be
dissipated to the night, but some
stayed to haunt the morning light."

COLETTE'S SHADOW

I

Thought Colette, at noon, her shadow crouched by her feet,
Fides, the dog: *shadow an echo of light, the street a drab*
with no fixed abode, passive by the impassioned Seine.

Still, the sun worries a cloud on its way and lowers
a globe of light to the asphalt, a sluggish dark river
meandering across the concrete that defines a city.

II

My shadow lies at my feet, a crouching monkey tired
of light. A spiral of chatter rattles the void: Bashōs frog.
Darkness doesn't fall. Rather, it rises out of its roots.

I stand in the shadow of my radiance, star-struck, held
by a night whose moon listens for the firefly's glow in
a silence which echoes the dark settling softly in place.

SWAN SONG

In the gulag, I, Ivan Dimitri
Golbanov, looked up only now and then.
Understand, the soup from the camp pigpen
was, as one might say, *le dernier cri*;
its flotsam of rotten cabbage, *a tout prix*,
(pardon my French), what mattered. If a hen
had crossed the ice-flecked mud, a dozen men
would have gutted it, and killed for the debris.
So when the birds flew over, on their way
to the warmth that held neither goad nor knout,
dreams of each night, and much of every day,
it meant only that winter was about
to pick over our dead flesh, feet of clay.
Every day, and night, I dreamed of baked trout.

GRENDEL'S DAM

she goes before,
her musk a wormhole burrowing air.

bloodspoor
splotches. she stands on the stone edge
her son stood on.

water parts for her incoming,
closes with pendulous flesh,
sluices off gobbets of tissue,
bits forgotten in a frenzy of flight,
as idly as a finger pokes
away a thread of lint.

Down through darkening comfort
she sinks,
becoming beautiful, scales
a net of gold
through which her
breasts
peer
no bigger
than a girl's.

On a deep ledge where she left him,
under a shoal of eager fins,
which flash to deeper darks
as she swoops, seal
to a watery charnel,
her arm-bereft son lies,
brute bones glowing
where skin and muscle
made way, a glitter of desire
parting the ways.

Here, she will wait for the one who follows,
his mail glittering like scales,
hair streaming upward

into the wake of bubbles
his coming will start,

eyes flooding the pool with light, with hate.

AFTER THE FLOOD

Albany Park, Chicago

so, there's this picture, the temptation of St. Anthony,
only it's done modern, the saint troubled by the flesh,
a young guy, a tattoo on his right arm, in a t-shirt,
and, oh, baby, what bubbies the tempter's got! she's
to his left, that's right from our point of view, mine,
looking at the picture as it stands against the wall,
but tilted back so it won't slide down, in my room.

I bought it from a guy with a Polish name years ago.
then, our house flooded, the neighborhood drowned.
we expected the government to wash its hands of us,
but it stepped up to the plate and, lo and behold!,
bit the bullet, declared us a national disaster area
and eligible for a SBA loan, which we didn't need,
and sent FEMA to provide relief, which most did.

anyway, this picture, a painting, oil-on-canvas,
shows the saint, looking petulant, sitting sort of
sideways in a wicker chair, and the girl cradles
a skull in both hands hanging down to her pubes
which are shadowed, and, therefore, indistinct,
by her arms and the chair edge, the light coming
from the street through a window behind them.

the painter's name is something like christ, only
with a slavic ending ringing like a carol. no beard
on the saint, just a kid oppressed by hormones in
conflict with the one church, which looms across
the street through the window behind him, a nice
touch, like the picture-within-a-picture, an icon,
Russian, at a guess, hung on the adjacent wall.

so this skinny kid looks away from the *zoftig*
creature who haunts his imagination, I guess.
I'm Jewish, after all, if an atheist, not privy to
church doctrine but alive to the arcana of the
incubus/succubus that sucks the subconscious

with a rueful smile. how the boy is putty in her
hands! how quietly he contemplates his fate.

for despite the success the church attributes to him,
necessarily, or consecration would be off the table,
the devil, as usual, is in the details, the pale taut
skin of a febrile young man useless as bloatware
beside this girl, a flush of estrogen signaling *ready,*
her body proof against what forbearance he may
bring to bear against the lust he cannot forswear.

THE POOP HE SAT IN

Maybe I ought to be writing about Ashbery, long in the tooth as he was then,
treading the wallows of democratic cliché, but here comes spring,
just when we all expected her, flaunting crocus and mildew
among the dumps of the downs.

                                    The tractor scurries across loam
turning up its nose at the turnips it turns up; the crocus croaks,
won't be still. Then is when I think why, oh why, my old dear, must we repeat,
like last night's leftovers coming up for air, that canard about (what?
jack jilts jill? oh, puhleeze!) any old thing?

                                    So it goes, as has been said,
admiring the luster a snail bequeaths to its path rollercoastering on
rails of sea-green snot. Or (go figure) we ride in that *beau* caboose,
(thank you, brother Stevens), cigar planted in the kisser
sloppy with desire, each of us a minor player who thinks
the crowd on the platform has come to offer us, well, not plaudits,
perhaps, but, at least, absolution, though for what we haven't a clue.

But, to get back to Little J.A., beguiling, i.e., gulling the riff and raff
who get off on a session of "Do you ashbery?" now and then, from
the settee tucked into the pile of Tabriz by the unwashed window.
Are they looking askance at Old Mother Cary who, counting her chickens,
passes in her frippery, light and loose, hollow bones
rattling the grim green table, stuttering her way to the fields
where Homer nods and the heroes wander among the spring flowers
they no longer remember amid the clangor of forgotten armor?

Meanwhile, and a very mean while it is, along comes light-hearted dusk,
heartless as old man frog baked into the enduring mud,
heartless, yet pregnant with the stone he bears unbearably,
head and heart entangled, and dusk is asking us to come out
to play, as the light, taking fright, is, puff-puff,
blowsily blowing itself away

petulant as petals...it may be

THE ROAD ON THE OTHER SIDE OF THE FIELD

How autumnal the field appears,
folded into mist too fine to see.

Last summer's grass waits for sun
to send a flush of green through dormant roots.
It takes an ashen pallor from the winter air.

A gray restraint infiltrates the yard
sapping color from a frieze of bush
scraggling past the railed-in porch,
an evergreen bolster for an earthen bed.

Well beyond the neighborly field,
the soil is studded with houses slicked by wet.

Now and then, a car will scurry along,
metal brow and chrome bobbing in unison.
Its fixed glass eyes glance our way
while it measures the road ahead
which goes, so far as we can tell, from
nowhere to nowhere else.

WILL MARXISM GIVE HEALTH TO THE SICK?

maybe it was the polio, which she had as a child, and which left its streaky mark
like a single fingernail
down her side corrupt as original sin

maybe it was the accident, the one that seemed to move slowly as a woman
sultry with heat across a room
toward the man who has taken her heart

maybe, just maybe, one doctor opined, it was that her back had not been right
since birth, since before birth, congenital scoliosis axing her axis

or, it might have been Diego, whose weight crushed her breasts which opened
like Indian offerings
spread on an altar to bleed his dark seed,

the pelvis crooked as Lombard Street in San Francisco where they lived in 1940
after they remarried and where he had painted *Treasure Island*

and they got along without sex, got along without sex with each other, though he
had his women and she lovers and her own deep-delving fingers

so wrenched out of true, her pelvic bore, she could not bear a child, though
accessible to the boneless tube
a man could thread into her, she willing

and she paints *My Nurse and I* in 1937, black hair framing a basalt mask behind
which the nurse's face
must lie whose features she has forgotten,

but she lies cradled in those brown arms, a seepage of milk from the left breast
trickling into her adult mouth, her child's body in a satin shorty

and helpless in those brown arms, as she was in Diego's embrace, and she
painted *My Birth*, earlier, 1932,
the adult head, as then, enhaloed by blood

resting on the white sheet, neck still stuck in the pelvic passage of the figure
covered from the breasts up
by a white cloth, and she painted herself

many times, with Fulang-Chang, her monkey, peering over her shoulder, or held
to her like a baby, or she festooned herself in tropical birds and set

vines and fruit alongside or as a backdrop for her almost-meeting eyebrows,
under which her obsidian eyes rivet the viewer and her scarlet lips

tighten, a clasp snapped shut, in contempt, or indifference, or holding in the
pain that flooded her being
until she could escape into the painting

you see, or another, perhaps *The Broken Column*, her body wreathed with
straps through which breasts
push, splayed out from a shattered marble

colonnade exposed by the torso torn open belly to throat, or the still life of
magnolias: heavy oil-green leaves, curls of white petals, stiff yellow stigma.

IN THE CAR AT THE DRIVE-IN BY THE SEWAGE PLANT OVER THE HILL

In the car at the drive-in
by the sewage plant
over the hill,
they thought about being in the car
at the drive-in by the sewage plant,
and the mosquitoes didn't matter,
the screen, which they watched in flickers,
between fingers, between spurts of too-warm beer,
didn't matter, and the 12:00 P.M. deadline faded to morning
where Sarah, Hazel, Beth with Steve, Perry, Joe
mingled their musky thighs
in the car at the drive-in by the sewage plant.

Now, they are all gone over the hill,
whose moment filled the back of an old Ford
with a whiplash flutter of tails, a coal oil
and sea-wrack odor,
who sent lint from the shoddy old man Ford
tacked onto the rib of each Tin Lizzie
confettiing the stumblebum air.
In the car at the drive-in by the sewage plant
where lovers rode tight as six-packs,
hustlers wrap their johns in marbled thighs.
Their tails go quick and sure as pistons,
eyes dead screens between features.

FLORIDIAN

A familiar like a loon,
or the thought of a loon,
the thought of the sound
a loon poised far off
on the edge of hearing
might make to the mind
musing on the mind.
Deep in the bayou, a
'gator roars. His bellow
works the mud, mangrove
sodden, where the
palmetto pirouettes. A
ghost passes on a passing
breeze, spreading hope
among the desolate
fronds that they might
feather another air
another time among
the blues for which
the sky is famous. Thus
a quiet settles among us,
an absence startling in
its intrusion, as though...
...almost as though...
a bronze bell woke us
striking the wrong hour.

PROFESSING DESIRE

"Without enemies!"

As the man said: "When we read, as often
as not, we remake the text to our image,
an image not of the author's making but of
our mistaking.   How, otherwise, explain
to myself, and to you, my surrogate, my reader?"

So, Roth. deep in the entrails of David Kepesh,
feeling for his liver, if only to check the color,
whether blotched yellow against a hectic field,
whether pustular and pitted, edges rimmed
by bands dense with granulomas, pocked
by hematomas, gray with cells that have
racked up a last stand at the O.K. Corral,
wrote what in print came to be: "Without focus,
without meaning--without a single friend! Making
only enemies!"   not, as I thought, merely "Without
enemies." [But this is not the point I mean to make.
That's coming up, scratched from the text's depth.]

How, one wonders, undo an error, one's misreading,
without going on the offensive, without pointing
out how much better the misreading than what
the page now plainly shows to the second sight?
(Ah, Hectic Reader, we're coming to the point.)

Ah, Kepesh! Ah, Roth! Caught in print not of your making,
a coded subtext right under your noses, one might say,
the problem being plain as the nose on your face,
as Father Kepesh might say, and poor David, no Goliath to slay,
having only *him[]elf,* **ahha! the careless reader lopped off his *s***

Ay, there's the rub, *Himmel Elfe* playing with himself,
the ghost of his mother crying, "David! Come out, now!
What are you doing in there so long?" as mothers say,
willfully unknowing what their boyish imp is up to,
ego bathed in testosterone, sister's panties making do, dubbing
the lines on the long wait for the real thing to come along,

as Kepesh might say. And so he roots around up there
(as once down there). Himself hell, he stokes interior fires
grammar will not excuse or exorcise...or

                              punctuation end?

DEAD TO RITES

AN ODE

In Grünbein's Manner

It was not on the road, where you might have expected it,
and it was not even it, whatever you thought it was,
the rag doll cylinder being had formerly animated,

but rested at the foot of a tree as though in homage,
half its fur intact despite the beaks starting work
and some of its guts hung over like a drunk at dawn

who hangs over a fence and rubs the sun from his eyes.
Once, half-grown, it had been caught neatly by a bumper
dipping into a depression in the road it had been traveling

and which lofted the ring-tailed passerby into Elysium
without so much as a by-your-leave. Now, the leaves
ready themselves to cover the remains when the birds

have done their job and the fur has fallen into the wind,
and the bones, the small white flutes, whistling their last,
have sent a fine dust of calcium dancing into oblivion.

ON BOARD THE HELEN H.

Sheepshead Bay

Cod slime freezes to slush
on the splintery deck.
The fish come up through black water,
break through the punishing air,
get hauled over a paint-chipped rail
in a tangle of line and ganged hook.

Pliers free the tough jaw
from the curved steel
stuck in an architrave of bone.
The gill cover gapes at the air.
The fish rise to engulf a chunk of
skewered quahaug adrift on a tide of chum.

Capt. Hansen steers into the wet,
January weather, into an Atlantic Cocytus,
where the cod maneuver through slate-dark cold.
It takes two hours to get to the banks
where the fish wait for our coming.
The hold stinks of fish scales and dried puke.

Into the burlap sacks headfirst
they go, sacks crusted with garum,
threaded brown-purple by gore,
the leftovers of last week, last year.
Abner Wilcox recorded that "A man might
walk to shore over ther backes, so

thicke they seemed," and "indifferent
to our hookes by wich we catched grete
numbers in the side or by ther tailes."
Melville's Ishmael eats with relish
a cod chowder, following one of clam,
two centuries later in New Bedford.

By the middle of the twentieth century
the shoals of cod uncountable were the stuff
of legend only, like the passenger pigeon
whose flocks numbered in the millions
and took hours to pass a given point
while hunters fired until the barrels

of their rifles grew too hot to hold,
and the feathered mounds drooled blood
onto the western prairies still stained
by buffalo shot from train windows by
travelers bound for the gold fields
and the rich tang of sure-fire fortunes.

Ice coats the rails and the bowsprit.
Down below, diesel fumes clog the throat.
Capt. Hansen listens to the ship-to-shore,
the banter of the other boats on the haul
out to the grounds to hand-line the gelid wet.
Morgan, the mate, chums off the starboard rail.

At the end of the day, we haul our haul
onto the dock, out to the waiting cars,
or we clean ten-pounders on the deck,
fling a gurry of guts and bone and heads
to gulls waiting for whatever booty sails
from the berthed boats back to the sea.

There is no end to the sea, we thought,
no end to the cod and herring, the eel
and ling, until the schools thinned out,
and the factory ships came back light.
The tonnage of dumped plastic, it's
said, may soon equal that of the fish.

TOVARICH!TOVARICH!TOVARICH!

the Red Army wound
in-and-out, a line of ants
stitching the fabric
of Mother Russia,

a million boots on the
face of the Motherland.
gray wolves shivered
on the taiga

White Russians
crying wolf
the tundra's far reaches,
and, in the many-domed

Kremlin, Ogpu
sifted answers lifted
out of the cold. the
weather turning ugly.

a flustered ptarmigan
clucked at the snow.
snowfall
covering up our mistakes

with its white chatter.
and the Red Army,
always on the march,
peppered the land

with the splendor
of empty uniforms,
and Cossack horses
quieter than snow.

in the huge distance,
we could see music
and the eyes of girls
calling us to order,

but their voices fade
into the sky, and even
the sky can't hold us
in its outstretched arms,

and the snow dampens
the western mountains
with its silent passage
and, turning, fades.

tovarich! don't leave me,
sounds over a landscape
history cannot fill,
nor myth tame.

SICKNESS

it's an old house with worn brick steps
leading up to the half-open door.

the sun ushering you up into the
mysterious hallway stops like a good dog.

it will wait on the stoop for your return,
if need be, partnering with its brother, night,

its light cloaked by a shroud of flannel,
its yellow face no longer turned to you.

inside, tendrils of being thread the gloom,
feverishly turn corners feeling for stairs.

sounds die, wings beating against drapery,
which hangs from unfathomable ceilings

fanning cobwebs of doubt and desire,
languorous hangerson of dolor and rue.

no two rooms smell the same though the same
whiff of rot stirs in the dust when you move.

you will inspect the recesses and alcoves
suspecting a nest of mice or a dead bird

until only your body, indolent and diseased,
remains, *however improbable*, as he said.

when you can't sleep, which is often,
you pursue the corridors that twist,

neither here, nor there, tired of entreaty.
there is another door, a back way, you find,

but it opens to a pitted slag field where
light grows exponentially less, a cone

of visibility petering out in defeat in no time.
if you are lucky, the front door will find you

(back to front, it may seem, its oldness
burnished as if to an unknown new).

for a while you will find yourself caught,
a period of scrabbling at walls sticky with damp,

beating away the chimeras of memory.
out of the miasmal dusk, the front door may

reappear, framed against the blank-eyed plaster,
and that good yellow dog welcome you back,

blinking and unsure, to a watery sky that acts
as though you'd never been away...if

FOLLOWING LOSS

...how loss is a great finding,
things you didn't know you had
pop up, invade the forebrain,
what you'd forgotten across the eternal mutter and clutter;
the painting that hung over the bed,
but at a tilt, before the flood washed it away,
hurried it down the street,
frame smashed against brick and concrete,
comes back to haunt you,
and the houses that stick up like stilts
pressed *voltafaccia* on familiar streets,
which you've never entered,
but remember,
the bed cradled in water,
the bed in which you'd spent so many lost hours,
and the desert painting in which a jackal, it might be,
stood beside a tent in a failing light.

...how could you have forgotten?
yet, now, you are unsure
whether the animal was yellow, or dun, or ocher
floating in the mauve air,
whether the tent flap slick as a spit curl
has been raised by a gust of air, or unseen hand,
through which the edge of an inlaid wooden table,
arabesques unclear, is what the eye unpeels from the paint,
or whether the silver spout of a coffee pot
about to fall to the floor
threw glints on the unfocussed eye before the bed was caught
in a swirl of water and taken into a past
you could not know would cradle your emerging being.
...so some mourn at the side of a dead fire
which ferried them into a place called *after,*
its bilges emptied into memory,
eyes fixed, or wandering in a cloud of unknowing,
prowling the corridors of *before,*
sparks lifted from the cobbles,
always a little too late to rescue the gilt horse

from its puddle of sintered metal,
to find the Egyptian poet's words
in this pile of ashes,
to pry a fragment of her smile
out of the jaws of death.

...and there are those who come into possession
of a great cache of ghosts that crowd the barrens
named *without* and which unfold into a horizon
they can never reach, and only with effort
recall, the sun graveled, sky pebbled gray-and-green,
memory a simulacrum of a time
in which loss does not exist,
a bubble clinging to skin,
over which existence washes,
and disappears, and, flows,
and, flowing,
disappears

DECOCTION

Three coffee beans rested uncomfortably
in a drain basket having fallen to the floor
and, soon after, been tossed into the sink.

One, the color of a shadow leaning on a wall
when the light is about to be silvery dusk,
spoke out of the despair of the forsaken:

Where the fruit bats make a tangle of sound
flutter among the forest trees under the moon,
I grew in the darkness of my sheltering husk;

I was made for better, I knew, or thought,
but for what? a small pellet of plant matter
roasted to this earthen brown, can I assume

my fate, or defy it, the horrendous steel
blades that wait below, the gulping gullet
that will lead to what infernal conclusion?

Another spoke of its time in the roasting
vat, jostled by a myriad others, its dark aroma
released into the chaos to what purpose none

could say. It spoke of the scoop which had
taken it up, stifled by a milling horde of
siblings, the fingers which picked and packed,

and the incarceration, waiting for shipment.
How it had sung to itself when it was freed!
How, abandoned, it had lost hope and faith.

Slightly off-center, against the slotted side
of the basket resting in a circular ring cut from
the porcelain sink, the third thought about

how the light from the window came through
like a bunched bundle of silken taffeta yellow

as summer-churned butter. It watched as the

hands of the woman went about their business,
the cutting of celery and carrot, unfolding the
fluted paper of the filter and the whirring cough

as the grinder made the beans small for the
water which would infiltrate the splayed grains.
It would not know the fragrance leached out of

its being but dreamt of what might have been,
of the long ecstatic moment waiting to be sipped,
to be savored in the dwindling moments of life,

at the end, fulfilled, to die unutterably drained,
not the ignominy of the ancient pipes leading to...?

Then, the countertop was swept of a few last
leafy bits. Then, the disposal started with a cough.

A FINAL MUSE

LEAVINGS
Bedford, MA

Was it a butterfly, or a flutter of air as ruffled
by an unseen hand? A fold of it went around
a leaf yellowing where the early frost reached
in, among a network of veins; a leafy rictus, its
cry would go unheeded and, indeed, unheard.

STONEFISH
Bora Bora

Looking through the water clear as cellophane,
he saw a rock, barely darker than the sea floor,
shift away, dislodging a ripple of sand, inches
from his shoeless foot, and he carefully stepped
back, away from the dorsal spine in its element.

THE END OF THE LINE
Wells' Time Machine

The sand stretches rubber band-like out where
a wintry sun the earth's dwindling rotation strips
of seasons lets its tepid heat breathe on the last
crustaceans, big as tanks. No wave scrapes the
lone and level sand free of the crossing tracks.

BIG AND SMALL
Out There

The dark energy implicit and the dark matter
explicit and sometime biding its time until. In
the long run, quanta churning out particles. *Now*
stretches a great way back. Further than you can
think: mv *here* embedded in there, you think?

mv=multiverse

A CYCLE IN THE CITY

In the city *ad se*, Korr sprawled now.
Heat was coming up from underslung stone,
sun in wane seeping through the afternoon.
Stone, drumming against belly and footpads,
whispered *nothing*; sea air awash out where
the stone stopped gave only departing scent,
the small sharptooth scurriers otherwards
leaving trailings of musk marking their *were*.
Eyes widen scoping a flutter of bug;
tongue coming uncoiled, makes a seeking road,
finds a roach waiting at the end of it.
The evening seepage from standing water
sends him back to his burrow in the stacks.
He leaves a nub of scat against the marble.

Korr sleeps, takes coolness inside from outside.
The shelf lends his smell its oily black self.
Skak can't slide up the vertical side slats:
rasps scale-on-scale on stone tasting for rats.
The air, too, stills, sleepy, perhaps, till warmed,
the onwards of a thing making it stir.
Stiff-winged bats slap fussing at the ceiling,
maybe. A confetti of sound rackets
from the walls unheard, sounds torn out of dreams.
Slowly, the night passes. Slowly, his heart,
having found the edge of darkness darker
than night, comes back. A lighter shade's
settling through the tunneling aisles.
He wakens to day starting up, above.

Vines grope the lions set on parapets.
A network of green veins tattoos shoulder
and thigh. The sun's inched up the sloping sky,
a mottled slug, its light a leakage
squeezed out of the bloated body.
Korr films his eyes, rebuffs the fractious dust
driven across an empty space by air,
dry thick drafts quarreling with the sun.

A leaf drops to the concrete, hunched crablike
till a gust takes it again from behind.
A line of blue ants makes its way across
undeterred by the stragglers Korr picks off.
An amethyst violence for a while's
hung overhead in a shimmer of wings.

The jac-spider, mole-brown-ticking her horned
carapace, jiggles an edge of web. Back
comes a flutter, a cabbage moth stuck
to the milky squirt of her spinnerets.
Korr nibbles a pigeon wing peppered orange,
a fester of mites anxious for leavings,
his crest lipping the syrupy air-waves
for packdogs' pong, the jangle of catshit.
A rattle of light hammers at the dome.
Rain bristles, rumbling across the city.
The spider moves on the web tethered to
a slab of stair twisted from its socket,
a bundle of juice-dense moth its being.
Korr rasps gristle knit to the creviced bone.

ASYLUM

"And why should I care?"
He said to the air
Caressing a toad,
Squat in the road
An egg sack its load.
A beak nearby crowed
Sharp as a goad.
The toad stood alone
Stiff as a bone,
Veined as a crone,
Then fattened to stone.
Of the bee as it mumbled
Its way across bramble
Hive-bound to a throne,
He murmured a moan,
"What's that to me?"
From the bear in the thicket,
Or ruminant beeves,
He would always take leave,
As likewise the cricket,
The chough and the pie,
As likewise the beaver,
And every deceiver.
The moon was his shelter.
He looked to the sky
From the fissure nearby,
The slag slabs and scree
Black as a smelter,
All lunar debris,
With a rigorous eye.
"What's that to me?"
He asked of the sea
Pockmarked, inert,
Dead to all hurt.
And the waterless lee
Forbore to answer,
The rock has no voice
To startle the ear.

See him still there,
Above or below us,
Bereft of all fuss
From bird or beast,
Freed by these walls
From all other calls.
Now less becomes least
Where someone sprawls
Contained in himself.
Look through the keyhole.
A cot and a shelf,
And stretched on the floor,
A shadow, no more.

ASYLUM, TOO

I have squirrels in my head
but most have gone to bed
and I hardly know that
they are there at all.

I don't hear them squeak or sing
but at times the nuts they fling
upon the waiting ground
say outside is the fall.

It's not the fall of man,
a hopeless also-ran
who races to acquire
or to maul.

It's the season's ring-a-dings
with winter in the wings,
and Time slowing slowing
always to a crawl,

and the sad and lonely case
embossed upon my face
which is blank and changeless
as though it were the wall.

So I stay without a word,
as though it were a bird
filling my head with some
melodious call,

and the inside happening
is a flicker of its wing
and the shadow is a
shadow, not a pall.

"THE QUESTION IS, 'WHICH IS
TO BE MASTER?"

"What shall we do?" the birdie said
to the little man who was not there.

And not being there, the little man
had no answer, and so he said so.

Then, they were on the edge of a pond, or,
when they were on the edge of a pond,

and the man and the bird had exchanged,
perhaps, a few words, or the bird had trilled

trying to lure the little man from a thicket of words
into the real world of crickets and pine nuts,

then, or, possibly, *when* that had occurred,
they came to a poignant conclusion. "Well,

that is nothing unusual," the little man said,
looking for attention, as usual, while I was

looking for a perspicuous figure of speech
as I was tying up the loose ends over here.

REPORT FROM THE SEA OF MOISTURE

The mocking-bird bush
squats under the riverbank
making a deposit.

It will grow, compounding all the way to the sea,
and the toadfish, which is real,
will swim disdainfully away
into the arms of the moon,

her ruby nipples fire stones,
her breasts edible oceans,

her flanks warm as yesterday's magma.

GOG TO MAGOG: A CREATION TALE

One day, he decided to build a computer as big as the universe. He had
not, admittedly, completed the universe as yet, but that posed no
problem. Beginning with the Big Bang, which he found nearly whole in
an abandoned lot back of whatever stood in for *place*
at the time, he added bits and pieces of being, a piece at a time, time
being one of the fictions whose service he found convenient from time to
time. "Sweat-equity," he would say, if asked, though he never was. Which
was reasonable enough given the paucity of parts in the as yet
unspacified primordial mush, a soup of dark energy, and its precursor,
nullity. When the mush had stiffened a bit and the first stars started
earning their keep, swinging in proto-elliptical orbits over the steaming
mess, he saw it was good, or good enough, and looking into the flux he
said, "Hell, yes!," already thinking about daubing in heaven and the other
place, a sort of sexual sandwich for the small spherical piece of shit he
had in mind for the evolution of giant ferns, whale sharks, gynormus
saurians, and the chimps and chumps branching out of the primate tree.
So he set that mechanism going and forgot all about it, about cosmic
residue due to irradiate the planet, curved space-time, hookworms, fossil
Lucy, food additives, the infamous Martian Mirage, and Pluto crapping
the pulp of tabloid papers on the lawns of a hundred towns. But I digress.
So, he built his mega-computer using quantum physics, which he
invented on the spot, to eliminate the need for germanium crystal.
Where to put it was, of course, a concern, but not a real problem for
something pretty close to infinitely capable, though he might have
smiled at "close to infinitely capable" as an absurdity, recognizing that
however great the power wielded by whatever he might be, it would
always be infinitely remote from infinitely anything. As he remarked,
parsing the Dedekind cut, "That's just the way it is," and got on with the
project. So, he built the universe in six or seven sometimes, and once it
was set set out to spin a humongous computer into being. Alas, for the
best laid plans of mice and so on. While he had been marshalling the
quarks and nameless bits of dark energy into something very like space,
the damn universe had expanded pushing actual space ahead of it, like a
cloudy fart, into being. How he had not foretold that remains one of the
great mysteries. Anyway, the supersupersupersuper$^{222222......}$ gran'daddy
of all PCs was falling behind faster and faster despite the nearly-infinite
(oops! same problem, but never mind) effort he was making to meet his
own quota. All this takes place long ago, in fact before then, and goes on

world without end, just as it is now. And we? we are a tick or a tock in the clock that keeps a record on the endless tape spinning unimaginably through the innards of that great apple ripening and ripening without the slightest awareness. Its role in the universe it is bringing into being is to keep on truckin', which, so far, it seems able to do. Should it ever (ha!) miss a trick, a tick or a tock, a grin of sand, grain of corn, and it will, the whole kit-and-kaboodle has been slated for cataclysmus, i.e., something very like an infinite dissolution, a dwindling, back to the drawing board and beyond and all that. Thereby hangs a tale, as the monkey said to his organ grinder.

RECAPITULATION

SOME OF THE GREATEST STORIES EVER TOLD

SOME OF THE GREATEST STORIES EVER TOLD: THE PREQUEL

SOME OF THE GREATEST STORIES EVER TOLD

in the beginning was the Void,
and it was unavoidable,
no way around it, no, no,
no WAY, José.

Thank God an anglo runs things.
He saw it wasn't so good,
nyah, nyah, nyah! a source of friction,
in a sense...ay, there's the rub.
Troubled by 'rhoids,
the celestial black hole of His anus
squeezed out a Bulge of Being,
which He shook forth into the Void,
which was unavoidable.
Oy, veh! what a *tumul.*

And He saw it still wasn't so good,
so he divided the *tumul*
into Jew and Goy,
sometimes known as dark and light,
and invented the light bulb,
and Lo!andBehold!
there was late-night tv,
six-packs, pepperoni pizza.

And Bill O'Reilly saw it was good
and said so on Fox News
and the people believed.

In the meantime,
and a very mean time it had come to be,
the home boys of Hebron got together
calling themselves Hamas
and buried the old warlord, Arafat,
on the mountain named for him,
where somebody named Moishe had cornered
the market on commandments
and somebody else had set them up

on the courthouse stairs,
which is another whole story,
come to think of it.

The lump squeezed out
in due course metastasized
driving the Void out of existence.
Those who had had the foresight to sell foreskins short
on the bourse in Frankfort, the market on Wall Street,
the exchange of Paris, London, Tel Aviv
made a killing of epic proportions,
and so it goes, prying the gun
out of their cold lifeless hands,
as another 'rhoid, now defunct,
was wont to say, a spray of his sputum
salinating the bland curds
of a post-modernist existence
away. So,

then, the Red Sea dried up
allowing the Israelites
to start the trek, for
Christ's sake, into the
second book of this,
excuse the expression,
Odyssey, with parables
and parallels, *bubbeleh,*
enow to fill up the void
which is unavoidable
though we've managed
to push it twenty-odd
billion light-years
away and it gets further
with each passing eon,
each millennium, each
year, hour, minute,
each nano-second that
bleeps somewhere in
a mountain in western
Colorado, but perhaps

that's another story.

Next week: GILGAMESH
AND THE QUANTUM KID

SOME OF THE GREATEST STORIES EVER TOLD: AFTER

*****^^^^^^^^^^+++++++--------####-------***------()()---------------------
----------------------------&&&&&&&&&&&&&&---------------------
--**--*
     * ____

----

etc.

NOTES

1. **From the Savannah Codex**--Poetry is, or may be, a creative art.
    In this poem, I envision a scene evoked by evidence from a highly
    complex world often, to most modern sensibilities, alien.
2. **Valéry Refracted**—An open-ended fantasy of existential fear and
    human hope. Each reader must find his or her way into, through,
    and out of the maze.
3. **Mudwomen**—In part, this poem is a kaleidoscope in language.
    In part, it uncovers something of the creative process as an alternating
    exploration and assessment. The entirety lightly touches on racial
    identity, social ritual, and changing ways of seeing what is merely
    a postcard.
4. **A Dream of Borges**—A sci-fi fantasy which plays with scientific
    terminology to create logically consistent and sensible descriptions
    of nonexistent imaginary places.
5. **Seams**—A simple poem about the clash of the mundane of life and
    conflicting feelings generated by ones realization of his mortality.
6. **A Battle at Sea**—A verbal realization of a scene on an ancient
    Greek krater with the poet's reflections on the thoughts/feelings
    the participants might have had, as though they were real.
7. **A Bloomsbury Portrait**—Reading Virginia Wolfe and about her,
    and about the somewhat introverted coterie of English snobs and
    artists, led to this wholly imagined picture of a scene from the
    late-Victorian world.
8. **Will Marxism Bring Happiness to the Poor**—Original title,
    "Will Marxism Give Health to the Sick," which change should
    suggest that Marxism isn't a part of the poem but a diversion.
    The poem is a meditation on the great painter, Frida Kahlo, wife
    of another great painter, Diego Rivera. I hope it suggests that an
    artist is an artist precisely because she makes new worlds, new
    sensations, new ways of being and seeing from her own experience,
    including those which are difficult and painful.
9. **Professing Desire**—An excuse to riff on another writer, this poem
    explores, to some extent, vagaries of writing, including punctuation,
    how writing and thinking interact to create worlds or introduce
    possibilities. It weaves in-and-out of Roth's mind/writing while
    making the reader aware of how the poet is, in turn, manipulating
    the meaning and world emerging from the subject writer's work.
10. ***Tovarich!Tovarich!Tovarich!***—"Comrade" in English. An attempt

to enter into the world of the Russian Revolution, the sweep of history, the desolation of war, the yearning need of the human for connection despite time and distance.

II. **A Cycle in the City**—Originally, a fantasy on a post-apocalyptic New York, the setting the famous library on 42nd Street. It might as easily be New York after Climate Change has flooded the city.

ACKNOWLEDGEMENTS

Some of these poems appeared previously as follows:

Colette's Shadow, *Illuminations*, Issue 33, Summer 2018
Report From The Sea Of Moisture, *Angry Old Man*, April 2018
Asylum, *Blood and Thunder*, Fall 2017
Floridian, *Kindred*, Spring/Summer, 2016
A Hillside In Wales, *Tule Review*, 2016
What We See, *Measure*, Vol. XI, Issue 2, 2016
Gog To Magog, *Hexagon Press*, May 2016
Will Marxism Give Health To The Sick?, *The Opiate*, Vol. 4, Winter
     2016 [since retitled]
Valéry Refracted, *Third Wednesday*, Vol. IX, No.12, Fall/Winter
     2015/2016
At The Border, *Clark Street*, Issue 96, Fall 2014
Willow, *Hurricane Review*, Vol. 1, Issue 10, 2013
Inuit Mollusc, *Idiom 23* (Australia), Vol. 14, Winger 2012
A Battle At Sea, *Etruscan News*, Winter 2012
Grendel's Dam, *Orbis* (England), #149, Autumn/Winter 2009 (an early,
     since revised, version)

My thanks to Kyle McCord, whose critical suggestions led me to
reshape a loose group of poems into a complexly structured book.

ABOUT ATMOSPHERE PRESS

Atmosphere Press is an independent, full-service publisher for excellent books in all genres and for all audiences. Learn more about what we do at atmospherepress.com.

We encourage you to check out some of Atmosphere's latest poetry releases, which are available at Amazon.com and via order from your local bookstore:

The Stargazers, poetry by James McKee

The Pretend Life, poetry by Michelle Brooks

Minnesota and Other Poems, poetry by Daniel N. Nelson

Interviews from the Last Days, sci-fi poetry by Christina Loraine

the oneness of Reality, poetry by Brock Mehler

Drop Dead Red, poetry by Elizabeth Carmer

Aging Without Grace, poetry by Sandra Fox Murphy

No Home Like a Raft, poetry by Martin Jon Porter

Mere Being, poetry by Barry D. Amis

They are Almost Invisible, poetry by Elizabeth Carmer

Auroras over Acadia, poetry by Paul Liebow

Transcendence, poetry and images by Vincent Bahar Towliat

Adrift, poetry by Kristy Peloquin

Time Do Not Stop, poetry by William Guest

Ghost Sentence, poetry by Mary Flanagan

What Outlives Us, poetry by Larry Levy

What I Cannot Abandon, poetry by William Guest

All the Dead Are Holy, poetry by Larry Levy

Who Are We: Man and Cosmology, poetry by William Guest